Sea Turtles:

Amazing

Giants

of the Sea

By K.S. Tankersley, Ph.D.

Little John Publishing

Kailua Kona, HI

Little John Publishing, a Division of Southwest Training
Development, Inc.,
75-5660 Kopiko St., Suite C7-157
Kailua Kona, HI 96740, U.S.A.

Paperback ISBN 13: 978-1493794362
and ISBN 10: 1493794361

Library of Congress Cataloging-in-Publication Data

Tankersley, K.S.
Sea Turtles: Amazing Giants of the Sea/K.S. Tankersley
   ISBN 13: 978-1493794362 and ISBN 10: 1493794362

Table of Contents

Introduction

Sea turtles are one of the oldest creatures on earth. They can be traced back to the time of the dinosaurs. They have been around for over 180 million years. Sea turtles are reptiles. Like other reptiles, they are cold-blooded animals that have a backbone, scaly skin, lungs and a three-chambered heart.

Sea turtles are found in all warm and temperate waters throughout the world. The smallest sea turtle is the Kemp's Ridley at 30 inches long (.762m). It weighs between 80–100 lbs. (36–45 kg). The largest species of sea turtle is the Leatherback. The Leatherback can grow to be over 6 to 7 feet long (1.83 to 2.2 m). It can weigh over 2000 lbs. (907 kg). Sea turtles live a long life. They can live to be around70 to 80 years old.

Seven Types of Sea Turtles

Sea turtles vary in color. They can be yellow, green or black depending on the species of sea turtle. There are seven different types of sea turtles. The 7 types are: the Loggerhead sea turtle, the Green sea turtle, the Hawksbill sea turtle, the Kemp's Ridley sea turtle, the Olive Ridley sea turtle, the Leatherback sea turtle and the Flatback sea turtle. The first six species of turtles are found in U.S. waters. The Flatback sea turtle is only found in the waters off of Australia and Papua New Guinea.

The Loggerhead

The Loggerhead sea turtle is found throughout the world. In North America, the Loggerhead sea turtle is commonly seen off the southeastern coast of the United States. Florida is the most common nesting site of Loggerhead turtles. It is also often seen in the Gulf of Mexico. It averages 28 to 37 inches (70–95 cm) in length and weighs 180 to 440 lbs. (80–200 kg). The Loggerhead is omnivorous. It likes to eat bottom feeding sea animals such as sponges, corals, sea worms, anemones, sea cucumbers, and fish eggs. It will even eat small, hatchling turtles of its own kind if it finds them swimming in the ocean. The

Loggerhead will also eat algae and vascular plants if it needs more food. Loggerhead turtles can be preyed upon by large sharks, seals and killer whales.

The Green Sea Turtle

The Green sea turtle is not named for the color of its shell. Its shell is usually brown or olive green in color.

It is called a Green turtle because of the green fat found beneath its carapace. Adult Green sea turtles have a length of between 31–44 inches (78–112 cm) and weigh between 150 –420 lbs. (68–190 kg). Green sea turtles are herbivores. They eat mainly algae and sea grasses. Young Green sea turtles will also eat soft sea animals like crabs, jellyfish and sponges when they find them. Most other types of sea turtles seldom come onto the beach except to nest and lay their eggs. The Green turtle does occasionally crawl up on a sandy beach to warm itself and to rest.

The Hawksbill Sea Turtle

The Hawksbill sea turtle is on the critically endangered list. Its shell has been used to make tortoise shell decorations. The Hawksbill gets its name because it has a long head with a beak-like mouth. The Hawksbill is mainly found in places with coral reefs. Divers often see themunder water resting in caves and on ledges around coral reefs. Hawksbill sea turtles are omnivorous.Their main food is the sea sponge but they eat algae too. They can grow to be around 3 feet in length (1 m) and weight around 180 lbs. (80kg).

The Kemp's Ridley Sea Turtle

The Kemp's Ridley sea turtle was named after a man named Richard Kemp. Kemp lived in Key West, Florida. He was the first person to send this type of turtle to Harvard University so it could be studied by the scientists there. The scientists named this new species of sea turtle after him. The Kemp's Ridley is a small sea turtle. It grows to 24 to 35 inches long (60–90

cm) and weighs about 100 lbs. (45 kg).
Kemp's Ridley sea turtles generally like
to live in warm ocean waters. They can
be seen on the eastern U.S. coast as far
north as New Jersey. They often travel
south into the Gulf of Mexico. The
Kemp's Ridley sea turtle is omnivorous.
It feeds on mollusks, crustaceans,
jellyfish, small fish, algae and seaweed.

The Olive Ridley Sea Turtle

The Olive Ridley sea turtle is a close
relative of the Kemp's Ridley. Like its
cousin, it isa small sea turtle with an
average length of about 2 to 2.5 feet
(62 – 70 cm). It can weigh up to 100
lbs. (45 kg). The Olive Ridley is named
for the greenish color of its skin and

carapace. It has a heart-shaped shell which is gray when the turtle is young.The shell turns olive green once the turtle is an adult. The Olive Ridley likes warm ocean water. It is found only in the southern Atlantic, the southern Pacific and in the Indian Ocean. The Olive Ridley prefers to eat creatures like jellyfish, snails, crabs and shrimp. It will also eat algae and seaweed if it cannot find enough shelled creatures to eat. Although it may have the biggest sea turtle population in our oceans, it is still on the world's endangered species list.

The Leatherback Sea Turtle

The Leatherback sea turtle, or Lute turtle as it is also called, is the largest type of sea turtle. It has a sleek, tear-drop shaped body. It has a large pair of front flippers made for fast swimming. The Leatherback turtle has the largest flippers in comparison to its body size of all of the sea turtles. In older turtles, the front flippers can grow to almost 9 feet (2.74 m) in length.

The Leatherback does not have a hard carapace. Instead of a hard shell, it has a thick, leathery skin with 7 raised ridges that run from its head to its tail. The Leatherback is 6-7 feet (1.83-2.2 m) long and weighs between 550 to 1,500 lbs. (250-700 kg.)

The Leatherback is found in more places around the world than any other sea turtle.It often migrates across the open ocean with its powerful flippers chasing its favorite dinner, the jelly fish.

The Flatback Sea Turtle

The Flatback sea turtle gets its name from the flatness of the turtle's carapace.The Flatback sea turtle is found in bays, lagoons, shallow, grassy waters and coral reefs off the northern coast of Australia and Papua New Guinea. Although it travels all around this ocean area, it only nests on the beaches of Australia.

Adult Flatback sea turtles can be just over 3 feet in length (99 cm) and can weigh around 200 lbs. (90 kg). They eat sea cucumbers, jellyfish, mollusks, shrimp and seaweed. Their carapace is olive-grey with touches of pale brown to yellow. The Flatback can also have white markings on the edges of its shell and flippers.

A Sea Turtle's Body

Sea turtles are built for fast swimming through the strong ocean currents withpowerful flippers instead of legs.Their flippers help them quickly swim through the waterat speeds of up to 15 miles per hour(24 km). Their backs are flatter than land turtleswhich helps them move smoothly through the water. Their front flippers act like paddles to gracefullynavigate the ocean waters. Sea turtles use their back feet like rudders on a boat. Their back feet help them steer as they move through the water. The female also uses her back feet to dig nests in the sand when it is time to lay her eggs.

Sea turtles are made for living in the ocean but they do need fresh water to drink. They have special glands which help them remove salt from the ocean water they drink.

Unlike land turtles, sea turtles cannot pull their head and legs inside their shells. They depend on their hard shells, large size and tough skin to protect themselves from predators.

Except for the Leatherback turtle, all sea turtles have a hard shell or carapace, covering the top part of their body. The scales on its shell are called scutes. The bottom shell covering their underbelly is called a plastron. The plastron is lighter in color than the top shell.Even though the leatherback does not have a hard shellas a carapace like the other sea turtles, it has many bony plates beneath its leatheryskin that can protect it from danger.

Sea turtles do not have teeth. Their jaw is more like a beak. In fact, the Hornbill sea turtle's mouth looks very much like a bird's beak.

Sea turtles do not have ears that we can see but they do have eardrums.

Their eardrums are covered by skin to protect them. Sea turtles do have a good sense of smell. They smell by taking in water and then pushing it back out. Sea turtles have good vision underwater but they do not see well out of the water.

A sea turtle is a mammal. It has lungs and breathes air. It holds its breath underwater just like humans do. Marine scientists believe that some turtles, like theGreen sea turtle, can hold its breath and stay under water for up 5 hours without coming to the top for air. How does it do this? While under water for long periods of time, the turtle's heart rate slows way down. Its heartmay only beatonce every 9 minutes. This helps the sea turtle save oxygen so it can stay under water longer. Eventually, it does need to come to the surface to get a fresh breath of air.

Even though they are able tostay under water for long periods of time, most sea turtles come to the surface about every 5 minutes when they are feeding

or just relaxing in shallow bays or
lagoons.

Sea turtles spend most of their day by
themselves. They swim, feedand rest.
Some, like the green turtle, do
occasionally climb onto the soft sand
to sunbathe and sleep but most prefer
to stay in the water. Most turtles
prefer to spend their time around

shallow waters, like bays and lagoons where they can easily find food and stay away from larger fish that might prey on them.

Sea turtles do travel through the deeper, open seasat times.When it is timeto go to their nesting beaches, female sea turtles will travel as much as 1,000 to 1,500 miles to get to their nesting beach. Scientists believe that for most turtle species,only the females go back on land when they are ready to lay their eggs. The males spend their time only in the water.

Nesting and Hatching

The turtle nesting season in the United States is between April and October. Female sea turtles mate at sea every second or third year of their lives. Once they have mated, they head to their nesting ground. Female sea turtles always return to the same beach where they were born to nest. When the female turtles are ready to lay their eggs in the sand, they use their back flippers to dig out a large hole. When they are finished laying their eggs, they cover their clutch of 70-150 eggs with sand. When the eggs are covered, the femalegoes back into the ocean leaving her eggs alone. The eggs, each the size of a ping pong ball, will stay in the sand for 6-10 weeks. In colder sands, the eggs take longer to hatch than they do in warmer sands.

The temperature of the sand where the eggs develop determines whether the babies will be male or female. If the temperature of the sand is below 85 degrees Fahrenheit (30° C) the babies are mostly born male. If the temperature of the sand is above 85 degrees Fahrenheit (30°C) then the babies are likely to be born female.

After the eggs hatch, the baby turtles, called hatchlings, may take up to a week to dig out of the sand. The babies come out at night andhead toward the ocean on their tiny legs.

Just after the baby turtles hatch is the most dangerous time in a turtle's life. Hatchlings use light and reflections from the moon to find their way to the water in the darkness. One of the greatest threats to the young hatchlings is lights visible from the beach. Lights from buildings and homes near the beach can confuse the hatchlings and cause them to crawl towards the artificial light and not crawl to the ocean. When this happens, most of the babies die. They might face hazards like animals or busy roads which could kill them.They may also die ofstarvation since there may be nothing for them to eat in the direction they are heading.

Man and animals can also harm the new hatchlings. People may take them because they are cute. Predators such as crabs and flocks of sea gulls may eat them as they are making their way to the ocean.

Even if the baby turtles make it into the water, there are many dangers in the ocean waiting for them. Larger fish and even other turtles might eat them. As a result of all of these problems, few of the babies will become adult turtles. Scientists believe that maybe only 1 of the many eggs the female turtle laid will actually become an adult turtle.

Endangered Sea Turtles

Of the 7 species of sea turtle, five are listed as "critically endangered" on the world'sEndangered Species list. The other two species are on the "moderately endangered" list.

There are national and state laws as well as international treaties

protecting the sea turtles. Even with this protection, sea turtles face many threats to their survival. These threats include loss of their nesting beaches due to development by the seaside. Another threat isillegal hunting of the turtles for their meat and their shells. Despite laws protecting the sea turtle, some cultures continue to kill them for their meat. They believe turtle meat isa delicacy. Poachers make a lot of money selling illegal turtle meat and shells to people who want them.

Turtles also face dangers such as boat propeller accidents.They might also get accidentally captured in fishing nets. When turtles get caught in fishing nets, they cannot surface for air. When they can no longer hold their breath they drown.This is a serious tragedy.

Another hazard threatening the sea turtle population is ocean pollution. Harsh chemicals, oil spills and trash in the ocean are another threat to the lives of these beautiful creatures. Since the mother lays her eggs and then leaves them, turtle eggs are also in danger. Both humans and other animals can become egg snatchers. This prevents the eggs from developing and hatching.

Areas that allow vehicles to drive on the beaches can also be a hazard to turtle eggs. Vehicles driving over buried turtle egg nests can destroy the fragile developing eggs as they drive across the sand.

Global warming may also be another threat to the survival of the sea turtle. Scientists believe that the warming of the oceans and the rising sea levels might also be dangerous for theworld's sea turtle population. Since warmer sands produce female hatchlings, scientists worry that there could be too many females and not enough males born to maintain the sea turtle population for future generations.

Sadly, as a result of these threats, the world's sea turtle population continues to decline.

Savingthe Sea Turtles

There are many things that we can doto help save the sea turtles of the world. We can keep our oceans and beaches clean and free of trash that might hurt the turtles. We can be aware of sea turtle nesting areas and stay awayfromhatching turtleswho are heading for the ocean. When we see turtles nesting on the beach, we can stay a respectful distance from them so that they can lay their eggs without fear. We can also tell our friends and relatives about how they too can help keep turtles safe and growing in number. This will allow us to enjoy the sea turtles in our oceans for generations to come.